AF366151

Meditation Book For Beginners: 15 Daily Strength Training & Home Workout Yoga Routines For Beginning Yogi Students

Juliana Baltimoore

Published by InfinitYou, 2017.

Yoga techniques and meditation work in cooperation to give you a feeling of inner peace and synchronicity. A rather more calm and relaxed existence will result from experiencing how meditation and Yoga connect and work together. You may walk away feeling refreshed and replenished from practicing the varied talents and strategies that a Yoga-Meditation connection is concerned with.

Yoga is awfully healing. It assists in handling prolonged discomfort issues and really decreases agony levels. Your muscles slacken up and your body is more pliable and flexible. The more use muscles get, the less distressing it's going to be to employ them.

Yoga abilities also coax the body to release natural analgesic treatments. You'll find that by practicing Yoga together with meditation methods will reduce hysteria and sensations of depression. Taking part in Yoga abilities essentially result in the body secreting hormones that may help the body deal with depression. Yoga is regarded as a natural mood enhancer so it'll relieve sensations of depression. It's also favorable in relieving uneasiness and the mixing of deep respiring exercises with muscle buttressing postures and the inside focus of meditation work miracles in improving how you are feeling.

Folks who practice Yoga techniques and meditation are way more focused and grounded and in charge of their bodies getting more conscious of their inner non secular self. You'll find that energy levels are increased.

Actually there are precise poses geared to extend energy and reduce sense of exhaustion and fatigue. In addition, the deep respiring exercises inspire oxygenation of inactive energy cells that can exist in the body.

The varied poses are toning and fortifying while simultaneously relaxing. This twin benefit aids in maintaining both a good mind and fit body. Yoga lowers blood pressure and improves circulation. Deep respiring boosts correct blood supply. The improved blood flow cleans the body and provides the desperately required oxygen flow. Muscles and other body parts need oxygen to function correctly and Yoga gives the muscles exactly that. Because both yogic techniques and meditation is focused on respiring, lung function visibly improves.

Respiration issues are relieved thanks to the controlled respiring exercises. Yoga classes regularly prescribed to heart patients as a sort of healing. Yoga cleans and heals the body moving you to a higher state of contentment. Over the passage of time practicing Yoga techniques and meditation teaches the mind to become uncluttered, calm, and balanced.

The goal is achieving a balance of mind, body and spirit which can better be accomplished when Yoga techniques and meditation are combined. The 2 much work side by side. The link of Yogic techniques and meditation systems offers many fitness and health benefits.

Yoga for health isn't a modern trend as some believe; the abundant benefits have been seriously aware about for over five thousand years. It keeps you in harmony with your body and mind in a selection of ways. Yoga techniques and meditation offer a unique balance which permits you to keep healthy and psychologically fit. Your body gets stronger and more flexible.

Pratyahara is turning your senses inward and letting go of the outside senses. It's a connection between the inside and outer forces of the spirit. The control over senses makes us achieve a bigger sense of appreciation of ourselves and the spirituality around us. Dharana fundamentally means targeting one thing.

It keeps the mind in a condition of attentiveness without any outside influences. It is required for Yoga to be well placed to hold the poses. Plenty of the Yoga poses are held for a lengthy period of time. The diverse limbs of Yoga work together and one leads into the other while also appearing to be connected.

Each breath should be uniformly drawn where you take in as much breath as you let out. Balanced respiring places you in a meditative state. Pranayama is debatably one of the most vital sides of yoga coaching. It really helps you transport to the place you have to be when doing Yoga.

These strongly related limbs work in cooperation to bring a condition of harmony to your being through the link of Yoga techniques and meditation. Dhyana involves the method of emptying your gourd. You noiselessly focus upon varied chakras or energy points in the body to gain a feeling of meditation and calm.

Meditation methods permit a user to let go. You're able to disengage your body from your thoughts to actually relax and discover tranquillity. Pranayama is focusing on each breath and directing it to where it must be so as to achieve the most benefits. You are basically respiring your life source.

The focus of meditation abilities is on clearing the mind. The focus of Yoga talents is on the physical contentment. Connected together the advantages are unlimited. There are both physical and psychological advantages to Yoga coaching when mixed with meditation practices. Meditation not only is related to Yoga, but it is basically a vital element of Yoga coaching.

Meditation is connected with the varied Yoga positions. The postures help you concentrate so that you can better benefit from both practices. It is an element of the psychological sides of Yoga that assist you to concentrate intently on what your body is doing. This brings about quietness of mind. It takes wonderful concentration levels to be well placed to do some of the more advanced poses in Yoga. Dhyana or meditation is amongst the limbs of Yoga. Some of the other heavy limbs are Pranayama which is the concentration on respiring, Pratyahara which is the withdrawal of senses and Dharana which is concentration.

If you practice Yoga, it is really important to learn how meditation and Yoga connect and what this Yoga-Meditation connection provides to your body. Being in a condition of meditation is being in a high state of Yoga. The link is a part of achieving a good life-style and religious accomplishment.

Fundamentally meditation assists you in getting the most from Yoga but it's so much more than that. The 2 states of spirituality are closely linked. Meditating will help you do Yoga better and doing Yoga gives you a better capability to meditate.

How Meditation And Yoga Connect

5 Minute Per Day
Yoga Routine

The Best Places And Times To Practice Yoga

jerrydownsphoto.com

Let's Do The
Yoga Moves...

jerrydownsphoto.com

JULIANA BALTIMOORE

PUBLISHERS NOTES

Disclaimer

This publication is intended to provide helpful and informative material. It is not intended to diagnose, treat, cure, or prevent any health problem or condition, nor is intended to replace the advice of a physician. No action should be taken solely on the contents of this book. Always consult your physician or qualified health-care professional on any matters regarding your health and before adopting any suggestions in this book or drawing inferences from it.

The author and publisher specifically disclaim all responsibility for any liability, loss or risk, personal or otherwise, which is incurred as a consequence, directly or indirectly, from the use or application of any contents of this book.

Any and all product names referenced within this book are the trademarks of their respective owners. None of these owners have sponsored, authorized, endorsed, or approved this book.

Always read all information provided by the manufacturers' product labels before using their products. The author and publisher are not responsible for claims made by manufacturers.

Copyright 2014 by InfinitYou

ALL RIGHTS RESERVED

One or more global copyright treaties protect the information in this book. This book is not intended to provide exact details or advice. This book is for informational purposes only. Author reserves the right to make any changes necessary to maintain the integrity of the information held within. This book is not presented as legal or accounting advice. All rights reserved, including the right of reproduction in whole or in part in any form. No parts of this book may be reproduced in any form without written permission of the copyright owner.

Favorite Yoga Quote

Knowing yourself is the beginning of all wisdom.—Aristotle

Introduction

Welcome to Turbaned Gurus, Sing-Song Mantras and Body Contortions? 15 Truth A Yoga Beginner Must Absolutely Know About Yoga. This is Volume 3 of this Yoga for beginners series. The third Volume includes 15 Yoga lessons and truths that a Yoga beginner should be aware of before even getting started.

My name is Juliana Baldec and I have been inspired by my sister Alecandra Baldec to get started with this wonderful discipline of Yoga.

I have been applying my daily yoga ritual for about three months now, but I still consider myself a Yoga beginner. I am so happy that I followed my big sister's suggestions to get started with this daily yoga ritual because it truly transformed my lifestyle, health and happiness.

I enjoy doing it so much that I decided to motivate and encourage other yoga beginners to get started with their own daily yoga ritual and routine, too.

Practicing yoga does not take much time out of your schedule, and if you'd like to learn some cool time management tricks that apply to a healthy lifestyle that includes disciplines like yoga and/or meditation then I highly recommend my sister's book series that you can find on the marketplace as well.

She also was the one who inspired me to write this beginner's Yoga book because beginners are always questioning her with the same type of ignorant questions and some of her yoga students even question the discipline of Yoga as a whole. She told me that the Yoga students who are beginners are very critical about everything that relates to Yoga and hence the title of the book: "Turbaned Gurus, Sing-Song Mantras and Body Contortions? 15 Truth A Yoga Beginner Must Absolutely Know About Yoga".

She gets questions like: "What are the true benefits of Yoga?" "Does it really work?", "Where does it come from?", "What exactly does it do for me?", "What are the differences of the techniques and poses?", "What is the best technique for a beginner?", "Can I beat stress with Yoga"?, etc.

Alecandra already writes books that are targeted to more advanced yoga and meditation techniques so this is how I got involved in this exciting book project and the book is designed to answer all the questions and shed truth on everything that a beginner should know about the wonderful and fascinating world of Yoga. All the answers that a Yoga beginner might ask in the beginning are answered as I go through each lesson. I have to cover over 30 lessons in order to answer the most critical questions and this is why I decided to make a series of this book. The first Volume is going to cover the first 11 lessons, the second Volume is going to cover the next 13 lessons and the third Volume is covering the remaining lessons.

There are other books that talk about Yoga for beginners, but the focus of this book is different because it does not talk about a certain Yoga topic in a boring, drawn out and long winded way, but it gives you a quick and snappy lesson to read and enjoy.

To make the reading process insightful and inspirational, I have also added some fascinating facts and stories about Yoga and I give you some of my own experiences at the end of each lesson. These are the most valuable nuggets that I have gotten out of my own daily Yoga ritual and I am considering myself a Yoga beginner so you might get some additional nuggets out of the book.

Each yoga lesson includes some inspirational stories that I personally associate with each aspect of yoga and takeaways that you must absolutely know about as a beginner.

The important thing is to get a quick overview of all the aspects that relate to Yoga so that you can make an informed decision about your own future with Yoga.

A beginner of Yoga only needs a short and inspirational lesson so that he or she is enabled and empowered to get started ASAP.

This book is designed for Yoga beginners who like to get started with Yoga but who do not know exactly where to get started yet.

This book helps clarify a confused mind or a mind with not enough information about Yoga. In short it gives you everything you need to know about Yoga before you are actually going to get into the action phase of Yoga itself.

I hope you enjoy the book and I hope that you will get lots of inspiration and mental stimulation out of the book in order to be able to take advantage of the unlimited benefits that you can achieve with this Yoga knowledge that you are going to discover as you go through the book.

Enjoy your journey through the wonderful world of Yoga!

Chapter 1: The World Of Tantric Yoga
"God, being Truth, is the one Light of all." - Adi Granth

Tantric Yoga illuminates the exaltation of the physical being more than anything. Tantra is thought to be the theory that emerges out of this type of dedication to oneself, which is the foundation of Tantra. The followers that believe in Tantric Yoga are called tantrics. These folk not only worship the physical condition and benefits that come from Tantra Yoga, but also the fact that they are empowered to reach any degree in order to delight the body and to reach occult powers.

As of this time, it isn't widely practiced and utilized in India. It survived only in some pieces of India in the middle of the jungles and hills of the Himalayas. Nonetheless, there are several clashes about its origin and source. Some have analyzed and learned that the Pre-Aryans are the originators and others transcribe it to the norms of the early folk.

It is understood to have risen at the very same time that Buddhism was blooming. Some Buddhists had incorporated and adopted some of the Tantric signs and symbols. Later it has grown to create a group or guild. Like the Vedas, Tantras are composed from collections of poems and verses that talk of the complicated strategies of the righteous and correct worship and devotion.

Curious Fact: Research does show that Yoga can really improve the sex activity and Yoga may even treat and prevent sex problems by increasing the overall health of our cardiovascular systems

Tantra Yoga, as translated by Shrii Shrii Anandamurti, is the practical philosophy which serves as foundation of Ananda Marga.

According to P.R. Sarkar's teachings, Tantra means liberation from darkness, the root tan meaning darkness, and tra liberation. Meditation is the primary non secular practice of this tantric convention, and through it the expert fights to overcome failings and defects. The root of Ananda Marga practice is covered by a group of rules called the 'Sixteen Points' that guide the Tantra Practitoner on both social and religious aspects.

Tantrism also involves the diffused way of taking mystical powers. It's also expounded that some tantric Yoga exercises aid and improve the general and sexual health. With healthy reproductive organs, one can have improved well being and it's propitious for sensual activities.

There are a number of Tantric exercises, both spiritual and physical which provide help in integrating the body, mind and soul into one single entity. These different exercises are good to start every day with and good before heading off to bed.

Through the exercise of Tantric Yoga, the physical functions of the body are excited and thus they help reactivate the entire well being of the individual who exercises Tantric Yoga.

The Most Holy Rite of the esoteric Tantric practice is the Chakra Sadhana whereby the Yogis and Yoginis combine with one another so as to accomplish the experience of Divine delight.

This is an account primarily based on a Tantric ritual as experienced in the Kamakhya mountains in the state of Assam, North Eastern India in the 1970's by Samaresh Bose. This convention is still practiced at Shri Kali Ashram.

"Five activities are crucial in the Tantric Yoga practice. These are known in the Tantras as the Pancha Makaras. These interpret as wine (madya), protein (mamsa), fish (matsya), desiccated grain (mudra) and sexual inclusion (maithuna).

These are the 5 sacraments that are characteristic of Tantric sadhana (Tantric praxis) .

In the tantric custom of Ananda Marga the religious aspirant (sadhaka) practices sadhana. Sadhana (a Sanskrit word) indicates the effort thru which somebody becomes absolutely realized.

In Tantra the non secular master, the guru, plays a special role. The guru guides and leads scholars on the religious trail. The aspirant learns meditation by a certified acarya. An acarya is most generally a priest or nun, but in the Ananda Marga convention there are "family acaryas".

In the initiation the aspirant makes a dedication to practice meditation and to live in step with the universal balance, and is then taught the strategy itself. The aspirant is then needed to keep the individual lessons private.

His system of yoga can be called as Rjadhirja Yoga, Tantra Yoga, or just Ananda Marga Yoga. The basic Ananda Marga meditation system is known as Sahaja Yoga ('simple yoga'). The sahaja system is composed of six meditation methods or lessons taught one at a time, on a private basis. There's also a set of higher meditation lessons taught to advanced practitioners committed to dedicate extra time for non secular practices and universal service.

Chapter 2: Tantric Yoga For The New Generation

"In the effulgent lotus of the heart dwells Braham, the Light of lights." - Mundaka Upanishad

Yoga is hip these days. With its diverse benefits, many are influenced to become involved in this kind of exercising and meditation. There are so very many sorts of Yoga that are known and practiced by many as of today. One if this is Tantra Yoga.

Tantra Yoga is more focused on the non secular healing and most of all the integration of the body, mind, and spirit.

In India, it's a traditional custom that sexuality is a very important and serious phase to be in a position to achieve a degree of enlightenment. In Western spiritual norms, sexual pleasures and needs aren't inclined or connected with spirituality. With these variations in practices, there exists a fine line between their feelings and approach toward sexuality together with spirituality. But in Eastern philosophy, they celebrate and rejoice on the grace and glory of creation.

Later, they have developed a study or science for knowing the best way to get the majority of this healing and excellent experience. Energy is understood and said to be the source of life in Tantra. Additionally, they consider the sexual energy and urge as great and holy energy.

Interesting Fact About Yoga: Research shows that Yoga can improve an orgasm. When an individual has an orgasm, the pelvic floor muscles which run between the legs do contract in a rapid way. The pelvic floor muscles are also known as moola bandha in Yoga. Yoga strengthens these pelvic floor muscles which provides benefits similar to the Kegel exercises.

There exists a couple of the various exercises that help in the performance of the sexual aspect as well as some nutritional alterations. A number of these physical exercises include contractions, respiring and holding certain positions. There are so many benefits that may be gotten out of Tantric Yoga by performing these assorted physical exercises. A number of these include improved prostate and functioning as well as reinforced and improved sexual performance.

Another benefit is improved sexual staying power when entering into sexual relations.

Apart from the physical exercises, there are psycho-spiritual exercises.

As a consequence, the pressure to perform and move is minimised.

Through mediation and correct Tantric Yoga exercises, one can think about the varied ways which will entirely satisfy the participating lover. When one is centered and focused on giving what the other lover actually wants, Tantric Yoga is an experience which can reinforce your relations with one another, additionally, you may receive the sense of satisfaction you have always dreamed of and maybe imagined in your sexual phantasies.

There are countless paths to take your foreplay to the top level. With tantric Yoga exercises and respiring techniques, healing massages and delicate caresses, one can receive a satisfying experience from Tantric Yoga that may excite the participating partners in a spiritual, physical and healing way.

Reiki or energy channeling healing is practiced before taking part in a sexual activity like Tantric Yoga.

Reiki is understood to increase the sexual pleasure in an intercourse. It's an Eastern healing art whereby one partner channels energy to the other participating partner. Healing is accomplished through tactil stimulation and activity and both the spiritual and the physical aspect are augmented.

In this fashion, the two participating partners can achieve a deeper state of relaxation and meditation which is extremely helpful for couples and partnerships.

Chapter 3: An Intro To Bikram Yoga

"Truth is one, paths are many." - Sri Swami Satchidananda

Many people do not really understand the deep meaning of Yoga, nor do they believe that they know about what benefits one really can achieve with Yoga. Until you've tried Yoga, it's impossible to know if you have got the kind of character that will actually excel under it's influence.

Yoga, very simply could be a life changing event and the discipline and psychological strength that come from it can utterly change your point of view and world view. One system of Yoga which is presently very hip is know as Bikram Yoga.

Bikram Yoga, frequently referred to as "Hot Yoga" follows the Bikram Yoga strategy. As with all Yoga, it has multiple goals to build up your inner strength as well as your outer strength. An imperative part of Bikram Yoga is the adaptability and balance needed to perform the exercises, and it's assumed this comes from psychological strength as much as physical practice.

The roots of Bikram are in Hatha Yoga, which is a healing Yoga form that is strengthening both mind and body. The creator of Bikram Yoga was Bikram Choudhury, a Yoga expert and trend setter. After a weight lifting accident Bikram Choudhury was striving to recover and set about inquiring into the healing capability of practicing specific sorts of exercises. The result was Bikram Yoga which so many folks revealed to be a good strategy of healing that it's users were recorded and passed on as a new Yoga style and Bikram Yoga was born.

Curious Fact About Yoga: Did you know that there are over 100 different Yoga schools. These do include Raja Yoga, Hatha Yoga, Jnana yoga, Bhakti Yoga, Karma Yoga, and Bikram Yoga. Each school of Yoga has different practices and routines, but they have one unified goal: the oneness with the universe and the state of pure bliss.

Actually there had been a patient who had a knee injury. He attempted to practice Bikram Yoga and just 6 weeks after constant practice, his knees started feeling better. Some problems and pains that he suffered from were all vanishing.

To become successful with the process of healing from Bikram Yoga, you want attention in practicing it. There are some folks who don't accept the advantages of Bikram Yoga. Bikram Choudhury developed Bikram Yoga with a bit of help from some scientists.

The scientists from the School of Tokyo School Surgery showed clearly that Bikram Yoga has medical benefits. Some of its advantages include the correcting of tissues helping in curing lingering infirmities. The discoveries and benefits were presented at the Global Medical Meeting in the year 1972. It was said that Bikram Yoga has the power to affect the body internally.

While Bikram was on his research at Tokyo College, he found out that the recovery process occurs when all of the body systems are working well, conditioned and braced.

Another Curious Fact: Did you know that Bikram Yoga is under big criticism from the larger Yoga communities for allegedly plagiarizing the true and traditional Hatha Yoga positions?

Those that practise Bikram Yoga solely for it's healing benefits are abundant, but there's also a robust holistic part, which is one of the important reasons behind using Bikram Yoga for lots of people who are regular practitioners.

The secret to success with Bikram Yoga is to develop the psychological strength needed to discipline yourself in it's use.

If you can master this side of Bikram Yoga then the physical benefits will be forthcoming and they've been proved by scientists including a group from the Tokyo Varsity Infirmary. The medical benefits are beyond question and have been demonstrated to improve protracted infirmities as well as significantly help in the treatment and recovery of tissue wounds.

At the 1972 Global Medical Meeting, the discoveries were presented and it was concluded that Bikram Yoga had the power to aid in the recovery of internal tissue. The rationale given was the positions practised by Bikram Yoga helped replace and replenish the cells and help in the lymphatic system flushing poisons from the body.

In addition to the poison and toxin drain the cells are assisted by higher oxygen flows during and after the exercise.

Bikram proved that to get the most benefits from the exercise a good and balanced body was vital. Where the body is weakest, Bikram Yoga will have less affect in the process of the recovery which depends on correct balance and circulation.

Bikram demonstrated twenty-six exercises and advised a regime, which was to be practised every day so as to best treat the body. Each posture exercise was developed primarily based on a background of both Western and Eastern Yoga disciplines. All of them target the movement and stress on muscles, nerves, ligaments glands and organs.

The exercises are supposed to be performed together and in sequence because they're all inter-related to one another. Bikram Yoga is low impact and can be performed by folk of all different ages. The vital part is the discipline needed to perform the posture exercises each day for max benefit.

Some poses are amassed with the mix of the eastern and western disciplines in Yoga which is focused on the stretching of the muscles, tendons, organs, nerves, glands and ligaments. The various postures have connections and each of it predates a posture that's beneficial in treating the body efficiently.

Anybody who would like to do Yoga can use Bikram Yoga. It selects no specific age group or age preference. This sort of Yoga works alongside a tourniquet effect which includes balancing, stretching and making pressure which is all done at a same time to keep a good blood flow to all of the parts of the body.

Thanks to Bikram Choudhury, the Bikram practitioner will now have solutions to today's raising medical issues and be able to stay healthy with a daily Bikram Yoga ritual.

Chapter 4: Experiences Learned From Dru Yoga

"Yoga began with the first person wanting to be healthy and happy all the time." - Sri Swami Satchidananda

Dru Yoga is a strong and stylish form of Yoga. It relies on directed respiring, soft flowing movements and visualisation. Its foundations were set in traditional yogic practice. Dru Yoga works on the body, spirit and mind. It improves pliability and strength, creates core stableness, builds an increased sense of positive thinking, is very relaxing and revives your whole being.

Dru Yoga was built to be practiced by folk of all different fitness levels, different capabilities and all age groupings.

This is a kind of Yoga that will swiftly get picked up or you can find out more about it by getting deeper into it.

Dru Meditation

If it's been one of your ambitions to discover how to meditate so as to feel that inner tranquility or to be a stress reliever, then try Dru Meditation works best in combination with Dru Yoga.

The Dru approach to meditation will help in bringing you balance regardless of what or how you feel. If you appear to be perturbed, Dru meditation will really help to bring you a sense of quietness. If you happen to feel exhausted, this type of meditation will give your energy. It'll bring peace to your spirit if you're feeling concerned.

The most vital benefit that the Dru meditation is going to do for you is to help you get in touch with that still place inside yourself, with its sense of fullness, accomplishment and deep curative properties that only Meditation and Yoga and in this case Dru Yoga and Dru Meditation in combination can bring.

Interesting Yoga Fact: The swastika is the Yoga symbol that doeas come from the Sanskrit term Svastik which means "that which is associated with well-being."

If you truly want to learn Dru meditation, the simplest way to do that is to go to a workshop or a meditation retreat in your neighborhood. If you aren't able to do that, you could try Dru meditation that can be found on CD.

You'll find that Dru meditation can help diminish fatigue and stress and bring you focus and calm.

Dru Yoga and Dru Meditation is the perfect solution for busy people.

Applying a combination of Dru Yoga and Dru Meditation is the perfect plan for you, if only you are able to do 10 minutes

(1x5 minutes Dru Yoga + 1x5 minutes Dru Meditation) daily of Yoga and Meditation combined.

It'll make a great difference.

If you are looking for a quick solution and if you are a busy Yoga beginner, please make sure to also check out chapter 15, Yoga For Business People, and the Bonus Lesson, The 5 Minute Yoga Ritua For Busy People.

Chapter 5: Hatha Yoga

"Tyaagat shaantir anantaram. The dedicated ever enjoy supreme peace." - Bhagavad Gita

Hatha Yoga is a traditional hindu system of working with the human nerve system. As it releases strain and endows one with replenished energy, many Yoga teachers have come to look on the venerable Indian physical science to find an exercise for health and energy of the body and spirit.

Hatha Yoga practices are way more religious than physical. Hatha Yoga is more a strategy of understanding than an unusual way to alleviate stress or loosen up the body. The sages who developed Hatha Yoga designed it as a technique to gain conscious control over our life energies. It is a method to go inside to harmonize the external so that our inner most self can be faced.

Hatha Yoga is about the states of consciousness, about living a divine life, and a way of preparation for meditation. As you perform the asanas, focus on feeling the energies in the nerve system. Sensitize yourself to knowing when the body has been in each position long enough to tune the nerve system that is concerned and then shift smoothly into the following asana.

It is like a dance, an intentional, liquid dance. During all postures, breathe utilizing the diaphragm, not the chest muscles.

Don't stretch overly or force the body. Relax into the poses. Do not be concerned if you can not perform them perfectly in the beginning.

Interesting Yoga Fact: The frequent synonyms of Yoga do include yoga-vid ("the knower of Yoga"), yukta ("the yoked one"), yogendra (from Yoga and indra) and meaning "lord", yoga-raj ("the king of Yoga").

It takes time and as you go with Hatha Yoga, you'll find your body getting more flexible and pliant. Free your mind of thoughts and tensions.

You'll be more aware, more alive, more unruffled. While there are a lot more complicated Hatha Yoga routines, a beginner should get started with the basic asanas (poses) which will give the beginner a good supply of exercises and a balanced system for everyday utilization.

For the easy point of quieting the mind in preparation for meditation, Hatha Yoga is all that you will ever need. For most satisfactory results, Hatha Yoga should be taught personally by a certified teacher.

These directions and drawings are meant only as a basic help. For more intricate programmes, inquire at a recognised college concentrating on Hatha Yoga. The scene of Hatha Yoga has a religious purpose - to balance physical and physic energies in preparation for meditation.

It's not only intended to make us young, stunning or creative, but to help us in quieting the mind, body and feelings that we may awaken enlightened consciousness & know ourself inside.

More Interesting Facts About Hatha Yoga: Did you know that Hatha yoga is the type of Yoga that is most frequently practiced and exercised in Western world. Ha means "sun" and tha means "moon," which represents Hatha Yoga's attempt to incorporate both complementary forces.

Chapter 6: Ashtanga Yoga

"A mind free from all disturbance is Yoga." - The Yoga Sutras of Patanjali

Ashtanga Yoga is a Yoga strategy that's taught in India by man named Sri K Pattabhi Jois. This form of Yoga involves the body's synchronization of respiring together with a progressive series of postures. Ashtanga is a method that produces some sort of intense internal heat as well as a cleansing and drenching sweat which helps the body and mind with detoxing the organs and muscles. The result is a robust and light body, a tranquil mind and an improved circulation.

Ashtanga Yoga Background

Ashtanga Yoga is a strategy of Yoga that was recorded by Vamana Rishi in a traditional manuscript call the Yoga Korunta. This document was expounded to contain inventories of a range of groupings of asanas and highly original teachings on the subjects of vinyasa, bandhas, drishti, mudras and philosophy.

The text of this document got handed down to Sri T. Krishnamacharya by his teacher Rama Mohan Brahmachari in the early 1900's. It later came into the possession of Pattabhi Jois when he studied with Krishnamacharya starting in 1927. Jois has been teaching this sort of Yoga since 1948 from his Yoga shala.

The literal meaning of Ashtanga Yoga is "eight-limbed" yoga as put forth by sage Patanjali. According to him, the trail of internal cleaning to expose the universal self is founded upon the following 8 non secular practices :

Yama which are moral codes

Niyama which is reliant on study and self-purification

Asana or posture

Pranayama which is controlled respiring

Pratyahara which is sense control

Dharana which is concentration

Dhyana which is meditation

Samadhi which is speculation Chapter thirty five

Astanga Vinyasa Yoga Astanga, or infrequently spelled Ashtanga Yoga is basically taught today by a person named Sri K. Pattabhi Jois, in Mysore, India.

He has brought Astanga Yoga to the west about twenty-five years back and still teaches today at 91 years old. Astanga Yoga commenced with the rediscovery of the traditional manuscript Yoga Korunta.

It describes a singular system of Hatha Yoga as practiced and made by the traditional sage Vamana Rishi. It is thought to be the first asana practiced intended by Patanjali.

The Yoga Korunta emphasises vinyasa, or breath-synchronized movement, where one practices a posture with explicit respiring patterns linked with it. This respiring system is named ujayyi pranayama, or the winning breath, and it's a technique that produces intense internal heat and a copious sweat that purifies and de-toxes the muscles and organs.

This also releases constructive hormones and nutriments, and is mostly massaged into the body. The breath guarantees efficient circulation of blood.

The result's improved circulation, a light and robust body and a peaceful mind. There's a correct sequence to follow when practicing Astanga yoga.

One must graduate from one sequence of postures to move onto the next. The Most Important Series (Yoga Chikitsa) cleanses and aligns the body, cleansing it so that poisons don't block.

The Intermediate Series (Nadi Shodhana) purifies the nerve system by opening and clearing the energy channels, permitting energy to move through simply. The Advanced Series A, B, C, and D (Sthira Bhaga) integrate the grace and staying power of the practice, which calls for intense pliability.

It is advisable to find a qualified and well informed teacher to help you through this discipline. It's an intense practice that's severe, 6 days every week. You are sure to find inner peace and accomplishment with each breath you take.

Chapter 7: The Ashtanga Yoga Technique

"I wish that the message of Peace may be experienced through Yoga, which is not only a culture of the body but the evolution of the Self." - Yogacharya B.K.S. Iyengar

Ashtanga Yoga is the kind of yoga which was developed and set up by K. Pattabhi Jois. This kind of yoga is sometimes known as the 8 Limb Yoga that has revolved in Pattanjali's giant concept. It presented the trail of purification is made from the 8 religious practices.

The 1st 4 limbs that represent Ashtanga Yoga are - Yama, Niyama, Asana and the Pranayama. These are regarded as cleaning practices which are outwardly curable. The other set of limbs which are the - Pratyahara, Dhyana, Dharana are the internal practies. These limbs can only ever be corrected by the right application of the Ashtanga Yoga technique.

This kind of Yoga technique is sort of deadly to the mind. K. Pattabhi Jois asserted that practicing these 8 Limbs and also its sub-limbs of the external practices which include the Niyama and Yama is impossible. By doing so, the body should be powerful so it can perform the practices sufficiently well.

If the body is feeble, and the sense organs aren't working well, practicing will never be handy in any way. This is a philosophy that K. Pattabhi Jois has applied and it is vital to understand so that in doing the practice, you are certain the body will improve.

Interesting Yoga Fact: A female Yoga practitioner is called a yogini and a male Yoga practitioner is called a yogi-this is a term which has also been applied to the 64 female deities who manifested the universal creative energy.

Vinsaya and Tristhana is practiced in Ashtanga Yoga. The Vinsaya is a fashion that makes Ashtanga and its beliefs distinct from the others. Vinsaya means the movement and respiring which is utilized for the internal cleaning process.

Each movement done is accompanied by only 1 breath. Sweat is the most vital product of Vinsaya. When you produce sweat, it only means you are successfully applying the practice. When you perform the Asanas, the body creates heat which causes your blood to boil and excrete the toxins outside of your body. The toxins are found in your sweat. So that the more sweat you create, the more toxins are released.

The poses are used to totally develop the strength and health of the body. The series of practices make this achievable. There are 3 postures utilized in Ashtaga Yoga. The 3 are classified on different levels. The 1st is the Number one Series which aims on aligning the body and also detoxing it.

The 2nd is the Intermediate Series opening and cleaning the energy channels which comes to the method of refining the nerve system.

The last series would be the Advanced Series from A to D. In this series, the grace and strength is measured.

The Tristhana is another Yoga principle which represents the union of the 3 places of action and attention. First is the posture, 2nd is the respiring method and last is the Dristhi of the Looking Place.

All of these 3 should work altogether to perform a function. Respiring methods are concurrent and synchronized. It is critical to make a single breath for one movement.

Ujjayi respiring is the Yoga respiring system utilized in the applying of Ashtanga Yoga. Applying this system must be extended after each practice. What you want to conquer is holding your pose longer at the exact same time. This is a dazzling respiring exercise which will boost your internal fire and will fortify your nerve system. Both Ashtanga and Tristhana handle the series of Dristhi. The Dristhi is referred to as the point on which you gain your focus or attention while doing the Asana.

This can enable your intellect to be purified and stabilised obviously. Setting the mind clear and cleaning it can only really be done in the Eight-Limb Yoga or Ashtanga Yoga.

Chapter 8: Need Power Try Power Yoga

"The yogi is superior to the ascetic; he is deemed superior even to those versed in sacred lore. The Yogi is superior even to those who perform action with some motive. Therefore, Arjuna, do you become a Yogi." - Gita VI.46

Core power Yoga is an energized Yoga exercise that physically and psychologically challenges to help connect to inner power without stopping and accompanied by a heated, climate controlled Vinyasa. It heals, de-toxes and excites the mind and body through balance and goal.

Power Yoga is a dynamic and challenging programme that mixes strength, sweat and spirituality. It recognizes power on different levels; first is the physical power which develops the body's strength and improve health; 2nd is the psychological power or the will to focus on the practice; and last the religious power which is the power behind the physical and psychological power.

Core Power Yoga is the Western version of the Indian Ashtanga Yoga

The term was was given by Beryl Bender Birch, an Ashtanga Yoga teacher. It's been brought to the west by fans of Sri K. Pattabhi Jois, a respected Sanskrit scholar who galvanized Western Yogis with his Ashtanga Yoga style and philosophies.

There are 3 programs in Power Yoga.

"Core Power" is meant to fortify abdominals and back and includes both abs-focused Vinyasa Power Yoga poses and adaptations of muscle-toning moves.

"Unlocking Athletic Power" will develop flexible strength with stress on abs, back, hips and pelvis.

"Soul of Strength" from the other viewpoint is a fast-paced Power Yoga programme with a definite 'mid-body" stress and some awfully challenging moves. Yoga sessions are done in a heated room and made up of different heart exercises planned to develop strength and adaptability, increase staying power, improves the facility to focus, release tensions and remove poisons through sweating.

Core power yoga practice also needs the execution of Yoga poses. Poses are done in a good rate, some poses are even held longer than the necessary 5 breaths. This practice can increase physical endurance and capability to focus upon any task for a long period of time without breaking the concentration. What is the disparity between core power yoga and other exercises?

Curious Yoga Fact: Scholars do believe that Rig-Veda ("the praise of knowledge") is one of the oldest known texts on earth. These texts contain elements of Yoga. The earliest hymns are believed to be more than 4,000 years old.

Core power Yoga is a vinyasa style that's got a unique programme offering and concentrates on core strength, balance and flow to build a solid practice based primarily on strength and spirit. It offers various classes like Hot Yoga, Yoga Sculpt, Bootcamps, Teacher Trainings and Mat Pilates.

The teachers of this exercise works together with his students to individualise their programs and making them feel that they belong to one community.

Power Yoga also offers excellent health benefits; this lengthens and stretches the muscles and at the exact same time it builds staying power, strength and lean muscle and mass. It also increases body heat that kills some bacteria and creates a well tuned state of consciousness of the actions of the body. The focus of core power Yoga is on the coordination of the breath movement, connecting the body, mind and soul to the highest level.

Core Power Yoga is best to those who need to improve their performance in their selected sports like cycling, soccer, swimming, skiing, surfing, running / sportsman, selfdefense skills and other team sports. Some coaching grounds in sports practice this exercise in transition for aerobics.

Core power Yoga can revamp your mind and body!

Chapter 9: Let's Do The Yoga Poses & Move

I do yoga, I do Bikram and I run, and I eat really healthy—Lady Gaga

Madonna does it. Cameron Diaz, Reese Witherspoon, Katie Holmes and Janet Jackson also do it. These famous celebs are working out the yoga moves. But this isn't why you must do yoga moves. The explanation that you must try the classical yoga moves is easy: It'll make you're feeling active with an over all good feeling.

Yoga is a traditional system of movements for private development of the body and mind. Yoga practitioners viewed it as an all-encompassing life-style, stressing compassion, non-violence and inner peace. It is composed of diverse yoga moves and poses. With its mild movements, yoga moves have been the ultimate technique for relaxation and body kick.

Furthermore, performing the yoga moves helps you stay targeted and awake during your work day. Like any exercise, you can do different yoga moves while sat at your desk. It also starts with the fundamentals of respiring. Nevertheless there are some yoga moves that are hard, but it is not critical to twist your body into any pose that is not comfortable for you.

Fascinating Yoga Fact: The Lotus position is a Yoga sitting pose that is meant to resemble the perfect beauty and symmetry of a lotus flower. Siddhartha Gautama who is the founder of Buddhism, and Shiva who is a major god in Hinduism, are typically both shown in the Lotus position.

Below are examples of the straightforward to do yoga moves:

1.The Downward- Facing Dog Pose

This yoga move is alleged to be the alpha dog of all poses. It starts with hands and knees. Spread your palms out with the pinkies about an in. from every side of your mat.

Press your hips up and back. Slowly lower your heels towards the floor.

Your body should be in a reversed "V" shape. Breathe efficiently, and focus on stretching your heels nearer to the ground, contracting your belly muscles and lifting your butt higher towards the sky. Make efforts to keep your head in accordance with your backbone by casting backwards towards your knees.

Stay in this position for roughly a minute.

2. The Tree Pose

This is an easy but forceful pose that requires balance and grace.

Stand straight with your legs together. Bend your left leg and place the left foot on the inside right thigh your left toes should point towards the floor and the left knee points out. With your hands on your hips, try and even them out so they're

more-or-less level and your body is facing straight ahead.

After you feel balanced place your hands in a prayer position in front of your chest and then slowly lift your arms above your head, keeping the palms together. Gawk softly at the point in front of you and inhale deeply, holding for roughly half a minute. Return to the beginning position and reverse legs.

3. Half Bridge Pose

Eventually, this pose will help you in improving your posture. Lie horizontal on your back with your arms at your side palms facing down, and knees bent with heels as near to your ass as practical. On an exhalation, push your feet and arms into the floor and lift your hips into the air so your butt rises off the ground and your quads are parallel to the floor.

Don't clench your cheeks but instead focus on extending your knees towards the wall in front of you, keeping your legs and feet parallel.

Roll your shoulders beneath you so your arms move towards one another and clasp your hands together. Stay in this pose for roughly a minute, releasing on a breathe out.

I only have one piece of advice for you and it is going to be the truth that you might not like to hear but it is the only truth and it applies for every new skill that you learn.

Practise, practis and practise even more!

Practise these yoga moves for a couple of weeks, and after the first weeks of practice you will truly see your progression. You will feel better and you will have lots more energy throughout the day.

If you practise correctly and on a daily basis you will be amazed of your achievement with Yoga. Couple your daily yoga workout with some other healthy drink and food choices and your body will reward you with unlimited health benefits!

Just do your Yoga ritual on a daily basis and start your fascinating path into the wonderful world of Yoga. You will soon discover some wonderful things that are going to happen on a physical and a mental level for you!

Chapter 9: Dahn Yoga For The Soul

"Peace is a quality of the soul. It fills the pure heart. Peace is in the heart of a desireless person who has controlled the senses and the mind." - Sri Swami Sivananda

Yoga is far-reaching and is steadily being developed today. Thousands of people around the planet are into this activity. Its influence is enormous and is continually enlarging. Of the so many types of Yoga, Hatha Yoga is by a large margin the commonest form. It can involve both the respiring control mechanism and the exercise and postures combined. This exercise permits optimised blood flow and improves one's suppleness, staying power, strength and vivacity.

Furthermore, it's also a type of relaxed mediation that makes a contribution to self-awareness and gives an additional energy that makes you have a positive point of view.

Let's take a look at yet another type of Yoga called Dhan Yoga. It is also known as Dahn Hak ot Dahnak. It started as an early type of Korean instruction programme that wants to teach the people concerning how to expand and broaden both the mind and body.

Interesting Fact About Yoga: Yoga is defined as having 8 limbs or branches. These are: Yama, Niyama, Asana, Pranayama, Pratyhara, Dharana, Dhyana, Samadhi. The 3rd limb, Asana, also refers to poses that most individuals think of when they are hearing the word "Yoga."

For a fixed period of time, it has been clearly demonstrated that it had disappeared but was later on re-discovered and its first center was established in Korea. It was in 1991 that Dahn Yoga was brought into the US. There additionally are existing centres there which have been established as time went by.

Dahn Yoga doesn't only target the fitness sides of Yoga. It also educates the individual on the guidelines and ideas on the way in which the energy acts or moves in the body. It also teaches that aging and weakening of the body is due to stress. And removing stress will certainly improve one's health and lengthen one's life.

Dahn Yoga supporters suspect that one should know the way to improve and develop the energy flow within the body. Through this, health is efficiently monitored and protected. With Dahn Yoga, one must know the way to communicate and correspond to one's physical body. The Dahn Yoga teachars also maintain that our body has its natural healing power.

Through deep stretching, respiring strategies and meditation, Dhan Yoga promotes physical, psychological, and religious healing and to attach us into our religious selves. It promotes body relaxation and the discovery of inner consciousness. It gives a life away and free from anxiety and stresses and a life that has self control and reinforced concentration. Through meditation and breath work, energy is amassed in the body. As a consequence, the working of the vital organs and systems in the body is augmented.

Additionally, the poisons and possible threats of disorder is obstructed in a way. Then the sensation of better physique and contentment is attained. This, in turn, boosts self-esteem and positive thinking. A new self is realized and freed from addictive behaviours. By the integration of the mind and body, latent capabilities are realized and goals are set. Additionally, Dahn Yoga practitioners occasionally volunteer teaching and coaching without payment.

Dahn Yoga is altogether a group that's pleased to encourage healthful contentment, a very contented mind, and a tranquil community.

Chapter 10: Drishti Yoga

"Follow your bliss." - Joseph Campbell

Yoga actually is a sort of exercise that came from some Eastern faiths, but it's also based mostly on mediation. You'll find the Yoga origins are interpreted in English from Sanskrit. When you're starting with your Yoga, you'll find that it could be a tricky time for you. You'll learn the power of Drishti once you've become an advanced student.

Most teachers will stress the Drishti will assist you in improving the way in which you carry yourself and your posture. You will be ready to get a clearer understanding of how Yoga works on the body and mind.

With the traditional Yoga teachers you may have heard stuff like wherever the stare lies, your attention follows. Ever heard the saying, "Keep your eye on the ball"? This is the same principle. In Yoga as a spiritual practice, as well as to benefit our health, the final goal is to calm the mind.

Yoga will help you to alleviate stress and you are your mind and body focus and see things more clearly. You'll find that it'll help you on a lot of levels. By fixing your eyes on a single point (a drishti), you can hone the abilities you want to bring your intellect to a single point, too.

Interesting Fact: The Swiss psychiatrist C. Jung was one of the first Western scholars who studie Yoga in depth. His comments and suggestions on developing a higher consciousness in the Eastern world helped introduce the Wester hemispere to the concepts and practices of Yoga.

Drishti attempts to block out external diversions so the mind is unconditionally concentrated on itself. When talking about Drishti, you'll want to learn the way to focus upon your respiring. If you keep an eye open as you meditate, you may also use an external source, like the top of you nose or the flame of a candle.

When practicing Yoga, simply select a point in the room on which to mend your gaze and your senses. You will be wanting to make certain you hone the skills you need in order to bring your mind to a single focal point.

This may be exceedingly helpful when holding poses for an extended period. For beginning Drishti Yogastudents, the Drishti will be the teacher. Remember that as you advance, your experience of the utilization of Drishti will advance too.

You shouldn't feel just like your eyes are strained or that Drishti Yoga does interfer without your Yoga routine. For people that are non secular, they'll see the activitiy as a technique to work on the mind and the body. You willl find that some types fo Yoga have some Drishti used poses.

You may try stuff like the downward facing dog and you may fix your stare on your navel. Your teachers will explain the utilisation of Drishti and the way to mix it in with your Yoga poses and your Yoga routine. They are going to tell you some suggestions on how it's possible for you to use your poses to help improve yourself overall.

Chapter 11: The Principle Behind Chakra Yoga

"The fragrance always remains on the hand that gives the rose." - Mahatma Gandhi

Your fitness is probably one of the most crucial things that you've got to look after. Due to this, plenty of people are doing all that they can solely to get the ideal balance of chemicals in their body so as to get the perfect health. You also have to consider that lots of individuals find it tough to stay cool and control their feelings.

You've got to remember that hate can make contributions to poor health and this is the emotion that you must decrease to a minimum. It is very important that you shouldn't be indignant in order to balance your non secular self and to achieve good health and good healing.

Today, a large number of people aren't collaborating in different types of meditation to achieve balance in their feelings and also in their spirit. You've got to consider that meditating can contribute to lots of substantial advantages and health benefits for your body. With meditation, you'll be in a position to relax more and you can effectively control your feelings and never be annoyed if you don't have to be annoyed. By not wasting your energy on negative things, you can put all of these negative energies and turn them into constructive energies that may come in handy in your day to day life.

Curious Facts About Yoga: Scholars and researchers believe that Yoga alos incorporated elements of the Stone Age shamanism. This dates back to at least 25,000 B. C. Yoga assimilated elements as transcendence, shamanic poses, illumination and asceticism.

Always recall that nothing uses up lots of energy more than annoyance. Therefore if you're having some problems controlling your feelings, issues in relaxing, or you only want to experience oneness with yourself, you have got to try Chakra meditation.

Chakra meditation is gaining in popularity today thanks to the health benefits it gives.

Not just that you'll have sounder health, but you may also live a more happy life with chakra meditation. It is exceedingly important that you need to do the

Chakra meditation everyday for a minimum of 30 mins every day to achieve religious healing as well as emotional steadiness.

Learning to do Chakra meditation is simple and everybody can do it. All you really need is a quiet room where you will not be troubled for no less than half an hour and some imagination and you are good to go.

First off, you've got to consider that there are 7 major chakras found in your body. These chakras are thought to be a crucial component of your body that has to be balanced to promote good health.

The 7 chakras are:

Shasrara (crown)

Ajna (between brows)

Vishudda (throat)

Anahata (heart)

Manipura (navel)

Svadisthana (sacral)

and Muladhara (root).

You must know how to open your 7 chakras to promote religious balance and good physical health. To do that, you have got to imagine a spinning light linked with each chakra. Start from Muladhara and work your way up to Shasrara. You must also know what colour of light is connected with each chakra.

Shasrara (crown)

Violet Ajna (brows)

Indigo Blue Vishudda (throat)

Light Blue Anahata (heart)

Emerald Green Manipura (navel)

Golden Yellow Svadisthana (sacral)

Orange Sahasrara at the top and being concerned with the pure consciousness

Red Muladhara at the bottom and being concerned with matter that is seen as gross or condensed consciousness

You need to also remember that it'll need the right respiring practices so as to successfully do Chakra meditation. These are a selection of the things you really have to know about Chakra meditation. If you would like to do this sort of meditation, you need to visit your closest Yoga instructor and they're going to teach you the correct way of doing Chakra meditation.

More Interesting Facts About Chakra Yoga: Did you know that the Yoga symbol "Om" is found in the Tibetan and philosophy? It is known to be the primordial sound of the wonderful universe and it is alos connected to the Ajna Chakra which is the conscience or also known as the "third eye" region.

Chapter 12: Yoga In Improving Personal Life

"There is nothing noble about being superior to some other man. The nobility is in being superior to your previous self." - Hindu Proverb

Yoga is a technique to escape from everything and go into your own tiny world. It'll help you to forget everything that is stressing you for a short time. Yoga will aid in making a positive change in your life. It builds pride, awareness, and focus.

There are numerous things that Yoga will help you with healing your mind and your body like depression and many medical health issues like Asthma.

Yoga is an ongoing treatment and you've got to stay with it to get anything out of it. You can't do it today and accelerate to get the full benefits out of it and then quit it after that.

What are the things Yoga will help you with?

Yoga can and will assist you with many things. You have got to stick to it and do it on a daily basis to get the full benefits out of Yoga. Yoga can be of help with respiring, so if your not respiring right, Yoga will teach you how it's possible to get in charge of your respiring.

Curious Fact: Most of the scholars agree that even though Hinduism and Yoga are very closely related, and that Yoga is within religion, Yoga is not itself a religion and Yoga is considered a type of spirituality.

Yoga will help you to learn the easy way to control your consciousness as well as your respiring.

In my case I was able to beat asthma because Yoga has taught me how to do the respiration technique the right way.

It will also help carpal tunnel, depression, lumbar region agony, multiple sclerosis, osteoarthritis of the knees, memory issues, heat illness, hypertension and weight loss. It will also help the elder individuals or individuals who have balance problems.

As you can see by now, Yoga can help you in many ways.

How to find out how to get started with Yoga?

You can go to your physiologist or chiropractor and these specialists will be able to tell you how it might be possible for you to be signed up to a specific Yoga programme that fits your health situation.

If they can't help you, you may want to try and go to your neighborhood library to find out some info regarding how to get enrolled into a Yoga class. You can also try your community college or the Learnin Annex. Check out the Learning Annex online to see if they offer Yoga classes in your local area.

Sometimes you might also be lucky and find a Meetup group next to you.

You can also do some searches online to find out what type of Yoga classes are located next to where you live. They have classes all over so you might be able to be enrolled.

I have also included a "Helpful Resource"s section in this book so that you can refer to more resources there.

Another option to learn more about Yoga is to learn via DVD lessons, interactive online courses, and books about the specific type of Yoga that you are choosing to learn more about and to get started with as a next step.

You can also check out my beginner's Yoga poses book that explains and shows the basic beginner Yoga poses. You can find more info at the back of this book.

Can Yoga hurt me?

Yoga can hurt you if you do not know what you are doing or you do way too much of it at once and as a beginner. That's why you have to speak with your doctor before starting anything new that might be too extreme or harmful to your body.

This is why you should choose the specific type of Yoga that you want to get started with wisely and with care.

You've to start slowly first pretty much like exercising you have got to build yourself up. You can not run right into any type of sports and expect full benefits from it immediately. It doesn't work that way. It needs time before you'll see any changes in your body or mind.

When learning how to do Yoga just take it slow and be conscious about it. Learn all you are able to learn because it'll assist you in dealing with a lot of health worries. Don't make an effort to do everything that is involved with the Yoga technique that you are going to choose at the same time and ensure that your chosen Yoga technique is ok for you to practise.

I suggest to visit your doctor, physician or chiropractor to get the ultimate guidance.

Then try and find a Yoga group that you feel positive about.

Yoga groups are always a good way to get started and that way you've got some support to turn to if you have got any issues. If you can not afford to pay for Yoga classes, try asking relatives and buddies to join together with you and get a group discount.

Make sure to check out the section "More Awesome Resources" in this book to find out more about the topic of discounts.

You can launch your own home Yoga exercising room. At local dollar stores, you'll find nice supplies for cozy decoration and maybe some discounted inspirational Yoga videos that you can add to your Yoga library at an affordable prize.

Use your book and video Yoga library to gain deeper abilities in Yoga exercises.

As you can see by now, Yoga is an engaging exercise. It helps you to develop muscles and alleviate stress. Yoga will help you loose weight, feel fitter and be more motivated and focused.

Generally speaking, Yoga gives you many options in improving your personal and your work life because it helps you get rid of stress and become a more positive person.

There is just one final step that you must do to achieve a lifestyle with Yoga and that is to get started today.

Please refer to the chapter "Action Steps" in order to get started today!

Chapter 13: The Best Places And Times To Practice Yoga

Deciding upon the number one place and the ideal time to practice Yoga is dependent on the balance that you specifically wish to achieve and attain. Numerous Yoga asanas help somebody to reach a carefully balanced spiritual Karma, psychological Karma and physical Karma.

There are standing poses like the "legs up the wall pose," that build strength in the lower mind and body as the feet are forcefully grounded. There are balancing asanas like the basic experience of the "balancing stick pose" and the "yoga tree pose," that are very good for coaching and training your minds to focus on goals and become better with mindset. The Yoga twist and turn positions, those practiced in Hatha and Bikram Yoga, do help in relieving strain and helping to free your body of poisons and toxins.

Yoga declutters the mind and helps purify the body of negative energy and toxins. Yoga practices also help to energize and stimulate the mind and body, as well as to calm our minds that may over flow with excited feelings and to balance and strengthen our body and muscular system. The perfect time to practice Yoga is when you have been practicing Yoga for a while. When Yoga is part of your lifestyle and your daily exercice ritual. When Yoga has been a fundamental element of your approach to life, then missing Yoga, even for one day, is going to be awfully obvious to you and you are going to miss your daily Yoga ritual.

For a beginner, Yoga can be practiced after good preparation. A Yoga beginner must be provided with valuable resources and a proper and practical Yoga guide that starts with the basics and helps a beginner with the Yoga positions for beginners. The most suitable time to perform Yoga exercices is when a beginner like you wishes to profit from the favorable effects of Yoga to cure the mind, the feelings, the body and the spirit.

As a beginner you must note that morning Yoga poses do result in an energy boost that's released to help carry you through the rest of your day. Stretches like the Sun Salutation poses and terminating poses like the Sukhasana loosens your muscles and relaxes your nerves.

The Pranayama poses and exercises permit your lungs to exchange old excess air for new air to fill them and to bring respiring staying power. This even works for Yoga beginners who suffer from lung sicknesses like COPD.

Yoga isn't a faith discipline; Practicing Yoga can be restricted to twice each day, relying totally on your own schedule. If you are able to engage in Yoga twice a day, then your results are going to be outstanding and fantastic! But if you can only perform one set of yoga poses a day, then that's fine, too and there's no need to work over on yourself as it defeats the effects and the purpose of what Yoga brings to your lifestyle. Yoga exercise sets in the afternoon is favorable if your morning is full of clutter and distraction.

Yoga poses and exercices performed in an environment like a nice bedroom that you like or outside in the park in the afternoon is a great physical and psychological booster and it is going to instantly energize you for the rest of your day.

Morning, evening or night time yoga exercices and movements are typically considered the most effective and suitable times to unwind and release all your tension and psychological and physical stress. Psychological strain can affect your sleeping patterns, too, and Yoga is an organic cure for sleeping disorders. Rather than sleeping with too much tense energy, with Yoga practices, you will be able to sleep throughout the night. You will wake up full of regenerating energy and restorative power and you will be able to start your day successfully.

Practicing straightforward asana and pranayama in the evening hours or during the night time, places your body and your spirit into a condition of relaxation and happiness. This produces a deeper sleep, releasing your body and spirit from any tensions that might build up in your body during sleeping.

Yoga is a very good discipline for your mind and your body, even if you are knackered, feeling excessively excited, tense or physically feeling achy or mentally sad. By performing 1 or 2 Yoga poses and maybe in conjunction with meditating exercices can make a very big difference globally, as your mind becomes more clear and more targeted and goal oriented. Yoga exercices and positions can be performed more successfully if your environment is quiet because a quiet environment will help with a better concentration and appreciation of yourself. This cognitive awareness also increases our other senses, for example your sensation of smell, explaining why a clean area is most fitted in practicing your daily Yoga ritual.

Yoga is amongst the most constructive exercise coaching systems for your experience and in order to perform a successful Yoga session you simply needs a Yoga mat and a towel. Yoga mats can be picked up in assorted colours, but the key is to discover a Yoga mat which is sturdy and doesn't cause any slipping or accident actions. Look for a Yoga mat which sticks to anti-slip properties and which absorbs sweat and which has sanitizing properties. Such Yoga mats are made specifically for Yoga practitioners. These Yoga mats are better fit for practicing yoga asanas. These Yoga travel mats are light-weight, yet extremely effective for practicing Svaroopa Yoga, too. Mats ought to be placed on a hard floor surface to stop the mat from pointlessly moving around as it could cause pointless injury to your body while you are doing your exercice.

Performing Yoga in a Yoga studio is the ideal location for all levels of Yoga practitioners. Such Yoga studios supply the ideal atmosphere required for successful chi results that you are looking for as a Yoga beginner. Yoga studios offer a spread of design styles for a singular self discovery journey for Yoga beginners.

Nevertheless, practicing yoga in the secrecy of your own home has developed into a more popular environment and many new Yoga practitioners prefer to stay at the privacy of their own homes. An in home Yoga space or Yoga room can be decorated specifically as a place for Yoga. Such a room may be rendered silent with some daylight streaming in in the daytime or a soft candle with a window which permits moonlight being admitted in order to create a very spiritual and enjoyable Yoga atmosphere. A home or a studio with a balcony or a patio is another great location to practice Mantra yoga, Anusara, Kripalu or Vinyasa asanas for a beginner.

You can also think about using additional aromatic candles and perfumes to help to realize a nirvana atmosphere for your Yoga ritual. Make sure to pick a perfume that isn't over powering neither is it a scented distraction so that you can stay focus on your Yoga exercices.

A home environment for practicing you daily Yoga ritual permits to quietly pose and move at your own speed. When you customize your own space and atmosphere, you can tailor your Yoga exercises to meet your express drishti wants. For both home Yoga practices, as well as in Yoga classes, time must be put aside to respire because a proper breathing ritual is part of a successful Yoga practice. Many Yoga scholars, both beginners, intermediates and advanced, play a role in outside Yoga sessions. It is a fact that Yoga scholars are prompted to practice welcoming their outside Yoga environment, instead of battling with the elements and diversions that are all around them. There do exist several Yoga poses that are favourable to senior Yoga practitioners, kid Yoga practitioners and pregnant women Yoga practitioners.

There are some other very interesting facts about Yoga. For example, it is a verifiable fact that the month of September is now called the countrywide Yoga Month.

The Dep. of Health and Human Services has delegated the month of September and the month of October 2013 as the months to help to educate and inspire folk to practice their entire bodies and to encourage individuals to get the most benefits out of a daily Yoga exercice.

Chapter 14: Cure Through Yoga

"Yoga is nirodha—the process of ending vritti-definitions of (which limit) citta-the field of consciousness." - The Yoga Sutras of Patanjali

One of the planet's oldest kinds of exercise is experiencing a rebirth in our nerve-wrangling modern world. You would not think that a 3000-year-old exercise could be beneficial for our health. Yoga truly is a cure and it is being prescribed by some medical experts for a variety of health illnesses and sicknesses. It is considered a cure against stress and to counterpoint other fitness schedules.

Talk to anyone that practises Yoga and they can speedily tell you a never-ending list of benefits. It appears that newbies speedily become converts to Yoga. They suspect it's the key to health and contentment in the modern-day world which today is a typical goal for the majority of people.

However, the best advert for Yoga is the indisputable fact that it appears to have graduated from the unusual and alternative ranks into a position of reasonably wide community approval. Housewives, businessmen, sportspeople, teens and the elderly are all practising an array of Yoga positions, meditation and associated respiring exercises.

For most Yoga becomes a lifestyle and a way of thinking.

Fans of Yoga like the integrated approach to fitness and health. Many pro sportsmen, hunting for the edge have become dependent on the power of Yoga as an extra kind of coaching. They've found that Yoga aids their state of psychological and physical relaxation between sessions.

Maybe one of Yoga's main attractions is that it mixes physical and psychological exercises. It is fantastic for posture and flexibleness, both key physical elements for most sports-people, and in some respects, there are strength advantages to be gained. Yoga teachers say the approach of Yoga care is probably one of the best techniques of achieving the psychological edge that sportsmen seek.

Curious Fact: Did you know that a York University research study found out that practicing Yoga reduced the physical and the psychological symptoms of chronic pain in women with fibromyalgia?

Marian Fenlon, for example, is one of Brisbane's leading Yoga teachers of the past twenty years and the writer of 2 books on the topic and has had thousands of Yoga students. A lot of them have, in turn, become teachers. Believe it or disbelieve it, she has even taught Yoga to footballers. Many years back, she took Brisbane Souths rugby league team for an eight-week course and, surprisingly, it was well-received. She asserts there are 8 parts to Yoga practice: perspectives, disciplines, posture and pliability, respiring, sensory awareness, concentration, speculation and meditation.

Yoga can play an important supporting role to modern medication, and complement other fitness and exercising schedules. While there isn't any great element of aerobic fitness in Yoga treatment, it enhances aerobics due to respiring strategies that may be learned.

So there are benefits for even the hardest of aerobic sports - swimming, cycling and running. There are countless documented cases of Yoga relieving or curing major illnesses - like Parkinson's illness, multiple sclerosis, coronary disease, and breathing diseases like asthma and emphysema.

Let's have a look how Yoga might be a helpful cure for a disease like asthma.

Asthma Cure And The Yoga Diet

To illustrate the point let me tell you how Yoga can cure problems of breathing and asthma.

One of the most useful methods to treat asthma attacks is through the Yoga diet. The perfect Yoga diet for asthmatic people are the consumption of pure or Sattvic foods. These foods are simply digested and not just that, but they're also awfully nutritive.

Most asthma patients are lacto-vegetarians. According to major researches, a paramount vegetarian diet is the simplest way to treat and control asthma attacks. The proteins contained in protein products are really hard to digest and so it burdens your metabolic system.

If you're not prepared to become a primary vegetarian, you can simply cut down your intake of red protein. After a little time, you'll get used to it and bit by bit, you can remove red protein from your diet. Being a paramount vegetarian has its advantage and it benefits asthma patients seriously.

You must also cut down your consumption of chicken, fish, and even eggs. If you're going to eat sea foods, don't fry them. You have to remember that asthmatics should limit their intake of fats, carbs, proteins but you can help yourself with fair sprouted grains, sprouts, green vegetables, beats, and fresh fruits. Try and eat more dried fruits like berries or oranges, black raisins, and prunes.

Make sure to have a satisfactory portions of tomatoes, beets, cucumber, lettuce, and carrots. It might be best to serve green veggies a little cooked or fried along with processed bread.

Another Interestin Yoga Cure Fact: Research studies do show that Yoga in fact reduces the risk of heart diseases by improving the arterial flow. Similarly, research studies show that Yoga helps treat asthma, diabetes and high blood pressure.

Asthmatics are also suggested to eat less to avoid pain. If you eat too much, you may feel just like you have overeaten or that you're over-full.

You have to take it slow while eating. Attempt to chew the food well and drink masses of water. When you're eating, try avoiding liquids as much as feasible and drink after you have finished eating. Like every other healthy individual, asthma patients desire satisfactory quantity of minerals and vitamins.

Vitamin A is impressive in treating asthma. You'll be able to find this vitamin in cantaloupe, squashes, sweet potatoes, pumpkin, carrots, apricots, pink grapefruit, spinach, and broccoli.

Fruits with intense colours contain high beta-carotene, so select your fruits well.

For hemoglobin formation and augmented autoimmune function, take a sufficient quantity of vitamin B6. You'll be able to find it in whole grains, fortified cereals and bread, fish, protein, eggs, legumes, nuts, and beans.

Have portions of apples, avocadoes, apricot, blackberries, blackcurrants, kiwi fruits, blueberries, pears, and peaches because these fruits are loaded in vitamin C.

So as to improve blood flow, get sufficient vitamin E. Attempt to eat spinach, olives, seeds, nuts, corn, wheat germ, asparagus, and leafy green plants. Plant oil is also important in your diet.

Roasted peanuts, walnuts, almonds, unsalted peanuts, mixed nuts, oatmeal, peas, raisin bran, baked beans, and dried peas are loaded in zinc which supports your adrenal glands. Selenium, necessary trans acids, and holy basil or tulsi are also critical.

The following foods can cause asthma: fish, eggs, shellfish, chocolate, milk, food additives, citrus fruits, and coloring.

To cut back the redness of the airways and get sufficient anti-oxidants, eat apples each day.

Dairy foods can also lead directly to excess mucus, to try and limit your intake of these products. Phlegm is doubly produced if you eat lots of sugar-rich foods, rice, pickles, iced drinks, ice, chutneys, and oily foods.

Avoid them so you can help the process of digestion.

My Own Experience With Curing Asthma Through Yoga

If you follow the right asthma diet and combine it together with a daily Yoga-Meditation ritual like I have been proven and tested it for the past three months, you will be empowered to beat these asthma attacks and decrease breathing problems.

Yoga and Meditation combined with my healthy fruit and vegetable smoothies and following the diet plan above has helped me reduce my breathing problems and my asthma attacks are almost gone.

I always consumed healthy food and smoothies before, but I have noticed a a much better result by combining it with Yoga. I feel fitter and healthier than ever before and my asthma attacks have become managable.

Yoga has turned me into a beliefer just like the individual in the story below who was told by everyone including doctors that he will never be cured. In reality he found his cure by practicing a daily Yoga ritual.

You can watch his inspirational story below and hopefully this clears up any remaining doubts or confusions that you might still have about the benefits and the effectiveness of Yoga as it relates to curing illnesses and diseases.

One More Cure Through Yoga

Here is yet another story how Yoga helped cure a very serious health problem:

Here is a very inspirational story of someone who was told by everyone and himself that he will never walk again, but one yoga teacher told him "yes you can!" and today he walks. It is a very inspirational story that proves the point of this chapter: Motivation is key to everything we want to achieve in life.

Yoga gives us back the power of motivation that we were already born with, but have lost over the years. This video proves that we are warriors and that everything comes from within us.

We only have to find back to the root and get in touch with our Motivation and then we are able to develop energetic will powers and we are unstoppable.

You are a warrior and a creator of your own destiny! Start with a similar powerful motivational mantra or however you want to call it and your day will automatically be filled with all the positive energies.

Start thinking like a warrior and start being a Warrior today!

Chapter 15: 5 Minute Yoga System For Busy People

If you are a buys yoga practitioner, I recommend the following yoga technique just before bedtime. If you have not done your daily meditation routine for the day, I recommend you take another 5 minutes and apply the 5 minute meditation trick that is explained in the chapter The New Age Meditation Technique. Take a nice shower and grab a herbal tea and finish your daily 5 minute meditation technique as explained above.

This 5 minute meditation technique is going to relax you and you are ready to get started with your 5 minute yoga routine. It is the perfect technique that you can apply after a nice 5 minute meditation session and before bedtime.

If you do not have enough time to do your regular meditation and yoga sessions during the day, these 5 minute routines are the perfect solution to still be able to lead a healthy and happy lifestyle that includes meditation and yoga. In order to truly reap the benefits of meditation and yoga for your mind and body, make sure to at least practice these effortless 5 minute meditation and yoga routines before bedtime.

If you apply these as instructed, you are truly leading a meditation & yoga lifestyle. It is critical to apply these two 5 minute routines at least once per day. If you do, your body, mind & soul will benefit from this lifestyle because you will be healthier, happier, and more relaxed and this is what I call a true meditation & yoga lifestyle!

Investing these 2x 5 minute routines will make your body and mind healthy, happy, intelligent, balanced, relaxed, and many more benefits that I can not all list here because there are way too many benefits that come from a meditation & yoga lifestyle. Not investing these 2x 5 minute routines will break your body and mind and your body. You will not be able to benefit from all these wonderful benefits that come from a meditation and yoga lifestyle.

So here comes the 5 minute yoga bedtime routine for busy yoga beginners.

Step 1:

Find yourself a very comfortable sitting position in your bed. Take a sitting position with your legs folded or with your legs straight in front of your body. Whatever sitting position that you can apply with ease. Lean slightly back and sit up on your backboard or pillow. Next, close both eyes and rest both hands on your thighs. Breathe for a few minutes in this comfortable position. This does not have to be a serious meditation routine. It is just for a short moment. Give your body a moment of pure breathing and nothing else.

Step 2:
The Twisted Sitting Position

Stay in this comfortable sitting position and twist around to the back of your bed. Do you have a backboard? If so, use your backboard and grab onto it to help your twist. Next, start breathing into the twist for a few breaths. Next, do the other side.

Step 3:
The Quick n'Easy Forward Bending Position

Keep your comfortable sitting position. Gently bend forward at your hips. Let both of your hands stretch out straight in front of you on your bed. This position will feel relaxing and very good in your hips and it will relax your whole back, too.

Step 4
Legs Extended Forward Position

Next, slowly start to straighten both of your legs in front of you on the bed. Keep your knees bent slightly. We are working towards going to sleep here instead of the power yoga moves that are better to practise during the day. Next, reach towards your feet with both or your knees bent. Keep your back flat at the same time. Next, bend both of your knees as much as you need to keep your back nice and stretched flat.

Step 5
Legs Extended Forward & Bend Round Back Position

You want to keep both of your legs extended out in front of your body. Round your back gently over both of your legs. This is a nice and relaxing stretch along your back's spine.

Step 6

Lying Down Knee to Chest Position

You want to roll back down on your back. Next, rest your head on your pillows. Bring one knee into your chest. Next, grab your shin to pull it closer to your body. Breathe for a few breaths. This breathing activity is going to lengthen your extended leg. It also it going to loosens up your hip. Next, switch legs and do the same activity for the other side.

Alternative: Do a Knee-Hug. Hug both of your knees into your chest. Use a slow rocking movement from side to side on your back.

Step 7
The Hamstring Stretch Position

Extend both of your leg straight up to the ceiling. Next, grab behind your knee or grab your ankle. Keep the leg straight. Next, slowly go ahead and start to bring your leg closer to your head and on each exhale. Next do the other side. Remember to be very gentle with these stretch movements. Doing it like this will help you drop any tension that is left in your body before going to sleep.

Step 8
The Half Happy Baby Position

You want to bend your knee again. Flex your foot to face the ceiling. Next, grab the outside of your foot and with the same arm as foot. It is important to bend your knee towards your armpit. You can do the same position with both of your feet at the same time if you like.

Step 9
The Bending Knee Lying Down Twist Position

Go ahead and bend your knee back into your chest. Twist your leg across your body. Next, turn your head into the opposite direction. Bring both of your arms out to a T-shape. Make sure to repeat the same exercise for the other side, too.

Step 10
The Star Shape Twist Position

Go ahead and extend your leg that is twisted over and reach with that foot out to the diagonal. Next, reach with your opposite hand to the opposite diagonal and go ahead and look towards your hand. This is a really nice and relaxing twist position. Next, repeat the same relaxing twist position for the other side.

Step 11
The Knee Hug Position

Next go ahead and hug both knees into your chest. Slowly rock side to side on your back. Make sure to let your whole back relax.

Step 12
The Savasana Position

You are almost finished with your daily yoga routine. Next, extend both of your legs out straight into a the Savasana position. Rest in the Savasana position for a while. Some yoga beginners prefer to keep this position and sleep in this position. If so, by now you are all set and you will have a very relaxing sleeping time throughout the night. When you wake up the next morning, you will feel very relaxed, energized, happy, and ready to get started a great day!

Step 13
The Sleeping Position

If you do not want to sleep in the Savasana position, go ahead and roll over on to your side, close your eyes, and enjoy a great night of relaxed and healthy sleep.

Easy & Effortlessly!

I told you all it takes is 5 minutes. You can easily repeat this each night before going to sleep.

If you can I welcome you to the wonderful world of the **Ultimate Yoga Lifestyle!**

Good night and have a wonderful & relaxing sleep!

Chapter 16: The Yoga Meditation Connection

Yoga and meditation work together to give you a sense of inner peace. A more calm and stress free existence will result from experiencing how meditation and yoga connect and work toether. You will walk away feeling refreshed and renewed from practicing the various skills and techniques involved in yoga.

Make sure to take at least 5 minutes out of your day and integrate some blissful meditation minutes into your daily lifestyle because not only will this benefit your Yoga routine in the long run, but a daily meditation practice will benefit your inner and outer self with in so many different ways.

Once you find your own way of zen which should be everyone's goal of the life journey, you will truly understand what is meant by this body mind connection because like everything in life you have to experience it for yourself in order to be able to attach meaning to it.

If you have not yet started your meditation journey, make sure to check out the second book that is included in this compilation because the meditation poems from A to Z called "Zen Is Like You" do help you with the discovery of meditation. They show you many ways of Zen so that you can go ahead and reflect upon them and get in touch with your own blissful way of Zen.

Action Steps

This is the end and I hope you learned some more interesting and intriguing truths about Yoga that you either did not know about or that you were confused about.

As a rule of thumb, I recommend to try out all types of Yoga because the more insight you are getting into each different type the better you will be able to find out the truth about each of them.

Each individual person is complex and we all are looking to achieve something different with Yoga. If you are looking to get a good overview of all of the types of Yoga, you will be empowered enough to find and match your favorite Yoga type to your own personality and situation.

On the other hand, you might be very inspired by a certain type of Yoga that has been coverd in this book, let's say Vini Yoga, because you feel that the benefits of Vini Yoga might match best with your preferences that you are looking for in a Yoga workout program. In this case it is the best way to get started with the specific Yoga technique right away and not to waste any time.

You can always read more and do more research about your favorite type of Yoga in order to become familiar with it on a very deep and intellectual level as you go through your Yoga journey.

The most important thing though is getting started and repeating the actual Yoga poses and the breathing techniques on a daily basis.

If you only have 5 minutes, go check out the 5 Minute Yoga Ritual For Busy People, but make sure to do it every day!

This is the only way that will bring you the quickest results and the best benefits with Yoga.

Just do your Yoga ritual on a daily basis and start your fascinating path into the wonderful world of Yoga. You will soon discover some wonderful things that are going to happen on a physical and a mental level for you.

Get started today and enjoy your newly found Yoga lifestyle and welcome to the wonderful world of Yoga!

To Your succuss with Yoga,
InfinitYou

Also by Juliana Baltimoore

Meditation Book For Beginners: 15 Daily Strength Training & Home Workout Yoga Routines For Beginning Yogi Students

Daily Meditation Beginner's Guide From Happines & Good Life to Stress Release, Relaxation, Healing, Weight Loss & Zen

Daily Yoga Routine Beginner's Guide For Happiness The Mindful & Healthy Lifestyle With Zen & Spiritual Eternity

Daily Meditation Eternity Prayer Poem Book For Positve Mindset, Motivation, Happiness, Success, Health & Relationships

Superfoods Recipes: Chicken Soup Recipes For Cold Recovery, Healthy Chicken Noodle Soup Recipes, Holistic Healing Chicken Recipes & Homemade Healing Noodle Soup With Chicken

31 Blender & Mixer Smoothie Recipes For Rapid Weight Loss

The Poetry Book For The Paleo Lifestyle

21 Green Fruit And Vegetable Smoothie Snacks: Green Fruit Yogurt Smoothies, Vegan Desserts & Herbal Veggie Bullet Blender Drinks

Blender Cookbook: 60 Blender Cocktails Recipes For Body Cleanse & Detox, Energy, Vitality & Rapid Weight Loss

Fasting Book For Health, Fitness, Weight Loss & Detoxing 11 Juicing For Beginners Recipes With delicious & Healthy Fruit & Vegetable Juices

Juicing Recipes Book For Vitality, Energy, Health And Fitness Nutrition 14 Healthy Clean Eating & Drinking Juice Cleanse Recipes

Smoothie Recipe Book To Gain Energy & Detox 17 Smoothie Bowl Recipes, Cleanse Drinks & Blender Mix Recipes To Feel Stronger

Fitness Cookbook: 60 Healthy Nutrition Blender Recipes, Vegan Gourmet Recipes, Juicing Drinks, Dessert Recipes & Healthy Ice Creams For Wellness, Health & Happiness

Juicing Recipe Book: 27 Epic Juice & Blender Recipes For Health, Detox, Weight Loss, Energy, Strength & Vitality

Scrumptious Paleo Desserts: Low Fat Low Cholesterol Dessert Recipes For A Healthy, Happy, Lean & Clean Eating Lifestyle
Weight Loss Juicing Recipe Book: Epic Juicer Mixer Blender Recipes For Loosing Body Fat, Body Cleansing & Detox

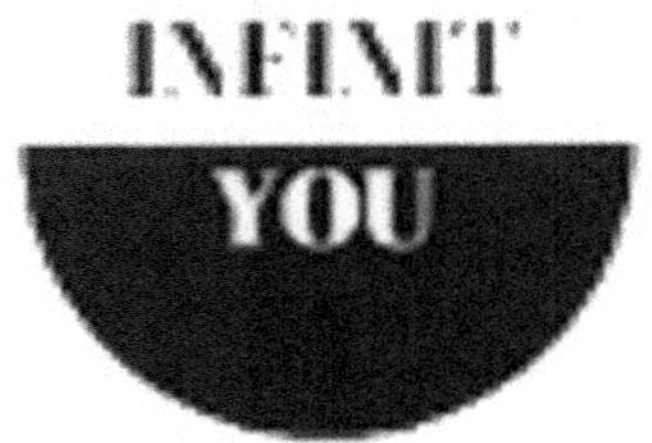

About the Publisher

InfinitYou is a hybrid general interest trade publisher. One of the first of its kind InfinitYou publishes physical books, electronic books, and audiobooks in various genres. Our publications are meant to educate, edify and entertain readers of all walks of life from babies to the elderly.Home to more than twenty imprints such as Infinit Baby, Infinit Kids, Infinit Girl, Infinit Boy, Infinit Coloring, Infinit Swear Words, Infinit Activities, Infinit Productivity, Infinit Cat, Infinit Dog, Infinit Love, Infinit Family, Infinit Survival, Infinit Health, Infinit Beauty, Infinit Spirituality, Infinit Lifestyle, Infinit Wealth, Infinit Romance, and lots more.

www.ingramcontent.com/pod-product-compliance
Lightning Source LLC
LaVergne TN
LVHW020348200726
843507LV00012B/2547